Become the Salt

How to Embrace Your Identity and
Experience New Life in Christ

Dr. Willie Bell Sublet Jr.

Copyright © 2021 by **Willie Bell Sublet Jr.**

All rights reserved. No part of this publication may be reproduced, distributed, or transmitted in any form or by any means, without prior written permission.

Unless otherwise noted, Scripture quotations are taken from the Holy Bible, New International Version®, NIV® Copyright © 1973, 1978, 1984, 2011 by Biblica, Inc.® Used by permission. All rights reserved worldwide.

Scripture quotations marked (NKJV) are taken from the New King James Version®. Copyright © 1982 by Thomas Nelson, Inc. Used by permission. All rights reserved.

Renown Publishing

Become the Salt / Willie Bell Sublet Jr.
ISBN-13: 978-1-952602-43-6

I would like to thank God for everything that has happened in my life to this point. I haven't liked everything, but I know that it was all to work out His will in me.

Thanks to my parents, Rev. Willie Bell Sublet Sr. and Dr. Abell Sublet, for their life lessons along the way. My dad went to glory in 2008, and I know that he would be proud of me. My mother is 89 years old at the time of the writing of this book, and she is so excited for me.

My sister Patsy Sublet-Quinn, the first published author in our family, has been my encouragement to share my God-gift with the world.

Special thanks to Deacon Edward Carl Johnson and Deacon Marzell Howell. These two men taught me how to study the Bible and seek God's face for life's journey. They have been there for me since 1984, the year I accepted Christ as my Savior, and they are still here to witness this blessing from God.

To my children—Vershun, Willie lll, William, Wendell, Mercedes, Lonnie, Maurice, and Ashley—I love you all. Thank you for your support of this project.

To the Sublets, Browns, Porters, McNeils, and Mitchells—I love the family God placed me in. You guys are great. To everyone who has encouraged me and those who have opposed me, thank you.

Thanks to True Believers Baptist, New El Bethel Baptist, Sure Foundation Bible Church, Miracle Temple Mission Church, and WE Community Fellowship. These church families all have a part in my spiritual growth.

CONTENTS

Foreword by Dr. Maurice and Dr. Priscilla Ricks 3
Passing the Salt 5
Complacency vs. Devotion 15
Changing Your Culture 27
Charitable Giving 35
Happy in God 43
A Reason for Praise 57
The God of the Impossible 65
Faith in Life's Battles 77
God's Power Against Our Sin 87
Resurrecting the Dead 97
Sharing Jesus 109
On the Winning Side 119
Notes 125
About the Author 127

FOREWORD

Foreword by Dr. Maurice and Dr. Priscilla Ricks

We are Drs. Maurice and Priscilla Ricks of the Sure Foundation Baptist Church, located at 8805 Fireside Drive in Dallas, Texas. We planted this church thirty-one years ago in our living room. Dr. Priscilla Ricks and I are also the founders of the School of the Scripture Accredited Bible Institute located at the same address as the church. The school was founded twenty-two years ago. We have been asked to write the foreword for Dr. Willie Sublet's newly written book about encouraging the saints within the body of Christ. We consider it a blessing from God to be asked to complete such a task.

Dr. Willie Sublet is a very special personal friend of ours. We have known him for over twenty years. We met him when he became a member of the Sure Foundation Baptist Church, and we have witnessed him grow in grace and in the knowledge our Lord and Savior Jesus Christ.

Dr. Sublet attended the Bible College and received his

master's degree and doctorate, and I had the privilege of attending both graduations. My wife and I consider him to be our spiritual son in the ministry. He has been instrumental in the spiritual and physical growth of the Sure Foundation Baptist Church in such areas as Sunday school and Bible study and as an instructor at the Bible Institute.

Dr. Sublet is a very gifted teacher, preacher, and pastor. He is a man who demands to be heard when he stands and shares the gospel of our Lord and Savior Jesus Christ. He is also a great encourager of the saints of God. As his pastor, I have had the opportunity to see this spiritual gift in action, and I can say with confidence that Dr. Sublet is the appropriate person to write a book on encouragement. After reading this book, you will learn how to encourage others as well as yourself.

Dr. Maurice & Dr. Priscilla Ricks
Pastor & First Lady

INTRODUCTION

Passing the Salt

Read Matthew 5.

At one point or another, we've all had an identity crisis. When we transition from adolescence to adulthood, we have an identity crisis because we're encountering unfamiliar circumstances and situations.

When we transition from singleness to marriage, we have an identity crisis because two people are becoming one. I had yet another identity crisis when I became a parent. Though I was excited to have a child, I had much to learn about being a father.

We also have an identity crisis in the body of Christ. We're meant to be salt, but many of us have lost our saltiness. Jesus said, "You are the salt of the earth. But if the salt loses its saltiness, how can it be made salty again? It is no longer good for anything, except to be thrown out and trampled underfoot" (Matthew 5:13).

Sometimes in our Christian journey, we lose our

saltiness because we've chosen to associate with people or lifestyles that slowly and subtly lead us away from Christ. In Matthew 5, the message is ultimately about the character of believers. If you don't know who you are (your identity), then it's going to be difficult, if not impossible, to recognize and challenge any unhealthy influences or habits in your life. To avoid unhealthy connections, we must identify ourselves with Christ and maintain our connection to Him.

More Than Salt Shakers

Back in the '60s, I lived in the city, but my daddy raised hogs. When he butchered the hogs, he packed them in salt to preserve the meat and keep it from spoiling. After he packed a hog down with salt, he hung it in the smokehouse. In biblical days, when people didn't have refrigeration, coating food with salt was likewise important for preservation.

The same goes for the world today in a spiritual sense: salt preserves. Matthew 5:13 indicates that we have a role as "the salt of the earth." We are to exemplify the Word of the living God in our daily lives. The world is like meat to us. Through Christ, we're supposed to be the coating of salt that preserves it spiritually so that it doesn't spoil in sin and disobedience.

Unfortunately, many of us in the church want to be mere salt shakers, adding enough spiritual salt to season the world lightly and enhance the flavor a bit as a quick fix, but not enough to preserve it for the long term. But Jesus didn't call us to be salt shakers.

Cure the meat! Pack it down. If you leave a spot uncovered, spoilage will occur in the house of God. A little sin can spread a long way, like a little yeast through a loaf of bread (1 Corinthians 5:6–8).

Have you let your witness spoil? Has the rot reached your marriage, your finances, or your health? When we fail to preserve our lives from spiritual spoilage, it tends to be a result of not truly desiring a life coated in Christ. Instead, we add a sprinkle of Jesus and then pass the salt. We avoid packing our lives in the fullness of the glory of God, because the preserving salt of Christ leads us to miss out on certain things of the flesh. As a result, we miss out on the kind of life He intends for us, and the world also misses out.

What does it look like to pass the salt?

Forgetting Who We Are

"I don't want to live only for Jesus, but I want to be saved to keep from going to hell, so pass the salt."

"I want to be part of a growing congregation that's serving God, but I don't want to do anything, so pass the salt."

Maybe you'll do everything you can not to identify yourself with Christ, because you don't understand your intended position.

> *But you are a chosen people, a royal priesthood, a holy nation, God's special possession, that you may declare the praises of him who called you out of darkness into his wonderful light. Once you were not a people, but now you are*

the people of God; once you had not received mercy, but now you have received mercy.
—*1 Peter 2:9-10*

When God moved you from the world, He gave you not only His mercy, grace, and love, but also His character. God puts us on display for the world to see who we are, but we want to know just enough about Jesus to get by. Do you know what that's called? Passing the salt.

Making Excuses for Sin

"I don't want my marriage to exemplify and glorify God. I just want to be married so I can finally fornicate under the pretense of marriage, so pass the salt."

"I want my children to be convicted about living for God, but they're smoking dope and having sex in my house. I tell them to pass the salt."

We've all asked people to pass the salt. "Don't pack me down," we say. "Don't call out all the dirt in my life with the Spirit of God. Pass the salt. Just sprinkle a little on me." You want to look like you know Jesus and talk like you know Jesus. But in your secret closet, you're bagging it up.

Young people in our society are looking up to us for vision and direction, and all we're showing them is how to pass the salt. What does your life look like? What does your marriage look like? Do you know that you're a Christian in your job, in your business? When you're in the grocery line, is there something identifiable about you when other people are bickering and cussing about how the line is slow, or are you one of those people?

> *Anyone who listens to the word but does not do what it says is like someone who looks at his face in a mirror and, after looking at himself, goes away and immediately forgets what he looks like.*
> —*James 1:23-24*

How many times have we walked into the body of Christ and rededicated our lives to Him, but as soon as we left the sanctuary or Bible study, we discovered that we didn't want to be patted down and preserved? We just wanted a sprinkle. We wanted the Word of God to justify our adulterous living.

Do you know that when we receive God as our Savior and then worship another god—like our car, our TV, or the ball game—we're committing adultery against the Lord? We won't see that if all we want is a sprinkle of salt.

Not Sharing the Hard Truth

"I don't want to tell this dying world that sin will lead to hell and destruction."

Remember that sodium chloride was used to pack down meat as a preservative. As "the salt of the earth" (Matthew 5:13), we are to preserve the world with the Word of the living God. Yet we go around, merely sprinkling salt on folks.

The world is telling us, "I see what you have, but all I

want you to do is pass the salt. I don't want you to pass it to me so I can be packed down and preserved in it. I just want a sprinkle."

We want to sprinkle just a little of Jesus on people who don't know Him at all. We're not trying to get their hearts right, because we're in the business of salt shaking. They don't want their good time to be spoiled, and instead of sharing the hard truth that can save them, we leave their lives to rot.

If you put a twenty-dollar bill in the hands of a toddler, he won't know its value. Likewise, some who claim to follow Jesus don't seem to grasp the value of His Word. The Bible says not to "cast your pearls before swine" (Matthew 7:6 NKJV). What do pigs know about handling the pearls of the Word of God? They don't see God's Word as precious.

How do you see the Word of God? Do you see it as something common or something precious? We put ourselves in danger when we forget what the Word of God says. We must value it if we are to preserve it, and we must share it if we are to serve as salt in this world.

Losing Our Saltiness

> *But if the salt loses its saltiness, how can it be made salty again?*
> *—Matthew 5:13*

It's difficult for sodium chloride to lose its taste, but if it does, then it's no good anymore. Have you ever sprinkled salt on something to change the taste, but the saltiness wasn't there? There was something wrong with that salt. How long did you have it?

How long have you proclaimed to be a Christian? How long has it been since you gave your marriage to the Lord? How long have you dedicated your children to the Lord and left them alone? How long have you neglected to give your business and job to the Lord?

Are you now trying to sprinkle some salt on these different areas of your life? Did you place God on a shelf until you thought that you needed a sprinkle of salt? God wants to pack you down in salt. A sprinkle is not enough.

Your salt shaking and your salt preserving may not be what you thought they were. You have to understand that if you're convicted by the living God, your character isn't like the world's. If you don't stand for something, you'll fall for anything.

Let God teach you how to pack folks down. Don't leave a spot uncovered. There's nothing we can experience in this life that the Word of God doesn't identify or tell us how to handle. Do you want to be packed down, or do you just want a sprinkle?

When we pass the salt, the world doesn't know what to do with it. We share the Word of God with people, but they don't even know that to be saved, they must confess with their mouths that Jesus is Lord and believe in their hearts that God raised Him from the dead (Romans 10:9).

All we want to do is show them our Christianity. We want to show them how much we know about the Bible, not about their situation. That's sprinkling the salt. If you don't know God, how can you identify your situation with a God principle?

Falling Away

We like to feel stuff. We don't want to be packed down, because it's a commitment. There's a lot of talk about how men don't want to commit, but the truth is that most people don't want to commit.

> *It is impossible for those who have once been enlightened, who have tasted the heavenly gift, who have shared in the Holy Spirit, who have tasted the goodness of the word of God and the powers of the coming age and who have fallen away, to be brought back to repentance. To their loss they are crucifying the Son of God all over again and subjecting him to public disgrace.*
> —**Hebrews 6:4-6**

God has given you the knowledge. He has placed you in a position to learn the Word of God, but perhaps you choose to stay away from the church. You live for your flesh. You please yourself with the world's goods. Then, when your body is broken down from reckless living, you may say, "Wait a minute. I need to change." You have destroyed your life. Christ can use what's left, but there's not much left to use.

When Christ doesn't bring you out of your sickness, depravity, mindset, or circumstances, you get mad at God. You blame Him and everybody else for your situation, but the fault lies in you!

What do you do when the mirror is looking at you but

you're not looking in the mirror? What do you do when your world is falling apart while you're still hanging on to your salt shaker? Some folks believe that the answer is in the salt shaker. They'll look at it and try to handle it a different way.

Back in the Eighties, we'd say, "When everything else fails, I go to the Rock." That's the wrong process. We wait until all of our other options have been exhausted. Then we want to pick up the salt shaker and sprinkle ourselves with the Word for two minutes, expecting all of our hopes to be realized. We don't live in a world of fantasy. We live in a world of reality. The sooner we realize that, the better our lives can be.

Preserving Our Witness

If salt is no longer salty, it's not "good for anything, except to be thrown out and trampled underfoot" (Matthew 5:13). God invented everything there is, but for good. Nothing that God did or does is bad. Evil resides only because good is absent. The destruction of our witness occurs when the salt is no longer any good because it has been contaminated. If we consume something that's been contaminated, it's harmful to us. The best thing we can do with it is throw it out. How many people have hurt themselves because of their contaminated understanding of the Word of God?

I don't want my witness destroyed. I don't want destruction to be in my mouth when I speak to someone about the Word of God and the goodness of the Savior. I want my life to reflect what I teach.

I believe that we pass the salt too much and don't tell the world what it really is, where it comes from, and what we're supposed to do with it. If we give principles to people who don't know God, it's like giving pearls to pigs. They don't know what to do with them. They don't understand the value or the purpose.

As Christians, we are the salt of the world. If the salt loses its saltiness, it's good for nothing. Its uniqueness and distinctiveness are gone. There's nothing left for it but to be thrown out and trampled. Likewise, when we lose our distinctive, Christlike character, we lose our purpose.

Are you going to be a salt sprinkler or a salt preservative? Allowing the Word of God to pack you down and preserve you from spoiling means that you turn to God first in all things. That willingness to trust God with yourself, your family, your business, your finances, your marriage, and your health will transform your life. The world will see a loving, gracious, and peace-seeking servant of God. This type of life changes the direction of the world.

CHAPTER ONE

Complacency vs. Devotion

> *Therefore, I urge you, brothers and sisters, in view of God's mercy, to offer your bodies as a living sacrifice, holy and pleasing to God—this is your true and proper worship. Do not conform to the pattern of this world, but be transformed by the renewing of your mind. Then you will be able to test and approve what God's will is—his good, pleasing and perfect will.*
> *—Romans 12:1-2*

God's presence in our hearts and our lives is meant to transform us from the inside out. His influence is powerful, and it's exciting! But we don't always see or experience that kind of exciting, transformative power in the church.

Some of us have been around church a long time. We've been around so long that we can go into any church in the United States and know exactly what's going to happen. ("Oh, he's going to close now. Now the prayer is going to start.") We get so comfortable with the routine that church no longer means anything to us.

Have you ever gotten burned out to the point where you don't want to go to church to worship? You may say, "I know what's going to happen there. I'm not feeling it. I'm not excited about what God is doing."

A Life of Complacency

There are two ways one can live. The first is a life of complacency. Some church folks know the procedure so well that they don't even get excited anymore about what God is doing in the lives of His creation.

Have you stopped reading the Word of God? Have you stopped praying to the living God? Have you stopped asking for an anointing? Because you stopped, everything else might have lost its meaning for you. You might have stopped feeling God's presence. Folks may not want to be around you anymore, because as soon as the pastor gets to the pulpit, you say, "I know what's going to happen."

The Dangerous Position of Complacency

When God can't show you anything new, He is probably trying to reveal something to your spirit. However, you may not see it, because you're stubborn and you've stopped praising God. You are in a prime position for a satanic attack.

Why would you serve a God who doesn't mean anything to you? Why would you keep coming back to a service if you know everything that's going to happen? Why would you give your talents in a place where nothing is new? Why are you sitting in church, listening to the gospel?

You may not feel God's presence, but God has done something in you that you can't experience elsewhere. You may even want more of God! However, at the same time, something inside of you has settled for a life of complacency. You may be saying, "I know what God is going to do if I do this. I know what's going to happen if I go my own way and don't listen to God. I know that the person I'm dating is unequally yoked with me, but I still want to be with them. I know that if I mess up, I can just ask God for forgiveness, and He will give me mercy."

It doesn't work that way. God forgives sin, but He still allows us to experience consequences. God warned you, but you went there anyway. You have to deal with the consequences yourself.

You may say, "I can do whatever I want to do, and just before my life ends, I can ask God to forgive me!" But do you know when your life will end? Why would He give you something so precious when you walked all over the blessings He already gave you?

No one will continue to give precious things to a child who consistently breaks them. God is saying, "When you lose connection with Me, you've pressed the pause button on your Christian growth." It doesn't matter what your age is, where you're from, or what degrees you have. What matters is your heart for God. Do you have a proud spirit? Are you complacent?

A Life of Complete Devotion

There is another way to live! You can choose to devote yourself to God and live for Him instead of yourself. What can you do to restore your intimacy with God?

Consider how you spend money. When you were in the world, there was nothing you couldn't afford. You'd go out and buy an entire outfit just for the weekend. You did what pleased you to satisfy you. But when it comes to investing in God's kingdom, you may tend to tighten up your wallet. If you think nothing of spending $130 for a dress or some shoes, why would you think twice about spending $50 on another Bible or a commentary to help you study? You spend money on games and other entertainment, so when it comes to spending money on the ministry of God, don't say that it's too expensive.

The same goes for how you use your time. If you regularly spend hours watching movies, shows, or sporting events, how can you say that you have no time for God? We make time for the things that are important to us. How much time do you give to Bible study, prayer, and serving in ministry?

God wants your time, tithes, and talents. He wants you to rearrange your priorities and put Him at the top. Romans 12:1 says, "Therefore, I urge you, brothers and sisters, in view of God's mercy, to offer your bodies as a living sacrifice, holy and pleasing to God—this is your true and proper worship." God calls us to a life of complete devotion to Him.

In View of God's Mercy

First, we need to recognize God's mercy. When we understand His mercy, we are more apt to follow Him. Then we need to repent of our lack of devotion: "God, I know that I haven't been what You require me to be. I know that I've been slacking in my study habits. I know that my prayer life doesn't exist anymore. I've been using the excuse that I can't really understand the Bible. It gets a little too technical for me. I don't really get those words. But those are just excuses. Lord, forgive me for my absence in fellowshipping with You and navigate me back to consistent study of Your Word. Thank You, God, for Your love and patience."

God is a merciful God, and we can come to Him with anything we are lacking. All we need to do is ask in faith, and God will grant our request in grace. We can come to Him in honesty and transparency because we know that He will respond with mercy and grace.

The Complete You

Like Uncle Sam, God wants you. He wants your social life, your marriage, your financial life, your business, your job, and your health. God wants all of you, the complete you. Present yourself as a living sacrifice. Rededicate yourself to the ministry of the living God.

I am reminded of a time, about three years ago, when trouble made camp in my marriage, ministry, and work. There was a mountain of pressure on me. I was supporting my family, studying to teach Sunday school, and studying to preach. I also directed the male chorus and the youth choir. All these things had me drowning.

The joy I used to have was lost. I would be in a worship service, with excitement about God's goodness all around me, but I felt nothing. My heart wasn't participating in the worship. I was going through the motions, but my spark was smothered by the pressure I felt.

I prayed and talked to my pastor about it. After that, God rekindled my joy, and I removed myself from some of those pressures. The lesson for me was to let nothing in this life cause me to pause in praising the living God. I want Him to have all of me always.

Holy and Pleasing

Be determined to allow God's holiness to spring from you to glorify Him. You are holy because God is holy. God has shared His holiness with you, so don't give God half-baked devotion. Don't give Him the little scraps that are left over after you've done everything else.

You may go through your day, doing whatever you want to do. Then, when the eleventh hour of the day comes, you decide to spend a little time with God. You say a prayer and turn to a familiar passage in Scripture—and your eyes close before you read five words.

There will come a time in ministry and in life when time to study won't be in your favor. Frustration will move in, and you'll become extremely unpleasant to be around. Pray for patience. If you push through these moments, God will give you a strength that you will never lose.

Reject Complacency for the Sake of Our Children

The complacent attitude has transferred to our children. They may be fifteen years old, but they think that they know everything about life. They may be thirteen years old and have a ten-year-old advising them about life: "Mommy and Daddy don't know anything. They can raise me, but they're not living in this world. They haven't caught up to the twenty-first century. They don't know what's going on anymore. They don't understand technology."

But when they knock their head on the door, whom do they run to? When they're in a serious relationship and unfamiliar emotions are running through them, whom do they run to? When they get themselves backed into a corner, with the ceiling coming down on them, whom do they run to? They don't run to the PlayStation. They don't run to the ten-year-old adviser. They run to you!

Sometimes we're so arrogant that we let our children stew in their messes. I'm so glad that the father of the prodigal son wasn't like that. When he saw his son coming down the road, he knew that his son was in bad condition and needed some compassion. The world had beaten up on him enough. The Bible says that the father didn't even wait for his son to get there. He ran to him, kissed him, and held a feast to celebrate his return (Luke 15:20–24).

There's a saying in the church that some Christians are so heavenly minded that they're no earthly good. Some people think that Christians' heads are in the clouds and we can't see the hurting people here on earth. We need to revamp our toolbox. We need to revise our approach.

I worked for GM from 1982 to 1993, when the GM plant in Arlington used to manufacture cars. But when the selling of cars began to decrease in some contexts in Texas, and many other people preferred to drive trucks, GM retooled their plant to make SUVs. Likewise, we need to retool our spirit to reach the kids of the twenty-first century. We need to retool our attitude to reach the families of the twenty-first century.

What we did forty years ago was good and fine, but we're living in a different day. That doesn't mean that if you were born in 1940, you can't communicate with people born in the '80s or the '90s. It just means that you have to spend a bit more time understanding who they are.

But if you're too wrapped up in complacency, you may say, "They aren't going to listen. I'm not wasting my time. I have tried and tried until my brain is fried. I'm not going to do it anymore."

You may be the last stand for those individuals! They're not getting Jesus at home, so you're their only hope! They're looking for someone to be dedicated and determined. They're looking for deliverance. Somebody has to stand up and show love, and that someone is you.

Choose a Life of Devotion

Get rid of the complacent attitude and choose a life of complete devotion. Rededicate yourself. Allow the Spirit to work through you to give glory to God. Be determined, and God will deliver you. Then you will worship Him wholeheartedly, and nothing anyone says or does to you will hinder your praise.

Say this aloud today: "If God doesn't show up, I'll stop breathing. If God doesn't show up, I don't have a new day. If God doesn't show up, the world has ended. The Lord has made this day, and I will rejoice and be glad in it. God, give me this day my daily bread. I'm not looking forward to tomorrow. I'm satisfied with today. If God gives me another day, I'm satisfied with that day."

WORKBOOK

Chapter One Questions

Question: Honestly examine your life. Are you living in a way that reveals your wholehearted devotion to God?

_____
_____
_____
_____
_____
_____
_____
_____
_____
_____
_____

Question: How do you spend your time? What does this reveal about where your priorities lie? Do you struggle with devoting time to God? Why? What changes can you make to how you spend your time to start pursuing growth in this area of your life?

_____
_____
_____
_____
_____
_____
_____
_____
_____

Action: Pray an honest prayer to God. Talk to Him about where you are, what you feel, and what you have or haven't done. Confess anything that needs to be confessed. Rededicate yourself to the ministry of the living God and allow Him to pour His mercy on you.

Chapter One Notes

CHAPTER TWO

Changing Your Culture

Read Ephesians 4:17–24.

If you travel to another country, you soon realize that it's not just the location that's different. You also have to adapt to an unfamiliar culture. Customs vary from one country to the next, and you may find that you've offended somebody without even knowing why! Even colors can have different meanings in different cultures. For example, in Brazil, the color purple indicates mourning or death while in certain countries in Africa, it represents royalty and wealth.[1]

When Paul wrote to the Christians in Ephesus, there were both Jews and Gentiles there. He explained the move out of the world into a life of Christianity. There's a change in your thought process and your mindset, which brings a change in your habits.

Since we have been changed and have given Christ our lives, we should no longer live by the culture from which God has delivered us. We no longer live according to the old ways of thinking, the old priorities, the old habits. This culture change is a process. We have to grow in understanding of the Christ-nature that's in us. God has given us His Spirit, who gives us instructions. When we let Him guide us, our lives transform from the inside out.

The Old Culture

How did Paul describe the old culture? He wrote, "They are darkened in their understanding and separated from the life of God because of the ignorance that is in them due to the hardening of their hearts" (Ephesians 4:18). People who don't know Christ have the lightbulb of their understanding turned off.

It isn't that they can't change or that God's Spirit isn't available to them. They refuse to allow God to change their hearts, so they lose touch with the truth of right and wrong. Some people do drugs, hurt their bodies, or steal from other people—and consider it to be fun.

In the next verse, Paul wrote, "Having lost all sensitivity, they have given themselves over to sensuality so as to indulge in every kind of impurity, and they are full of greed" (Ephesians 4:19). Because of the hardening of their hearts, they've given themselves over to all sorts of impure acts. As long as they are pleasing themselves, it doesn't matter to them what they do. This is a continual process of how low one can go. They keep lowering their standards, looking for the next thrill.

Many children are brought up in families of hatred. When they're introduced to Jesus, it challenges in a very powerful way what they've been raised to believe. When you're challenged in these ways and your mindset changes, it should bring tears to your eyes. There should be remorse in your spirit as you ask yourself, "How can I think like that? How can I continue to hurt people and think it's okay?"

A New Culture

> *That, however, is not the way of life you learned when you heard about Christ and were taught in him in accordance with the truth that is in Jesus.*
> —**Ephesians 4:20–21**

You didn't follow your own thought process and devious, impure acts to get to Christ. That type of thinking didn't lead you to Christ. That type of thinking will lead you to prison.

When you receive the truth and the salvation of Christ, you are accepted into a different culture, and you need to learn how to behave in it. The light has been turned on, and you no longer live in darkness. The law of Jesus, the law of love, has proven to you that your old way of thinking was warped. Things need to change, and if they don't change, it's a sign that your heart has hardened.

How Do We Live Out the New Culture?

Paul wrote, "You were taught, with regard to your former way of life, to put off your old self, which is being corrupted by its deceitful desires; to be made new in the attitude of your minds" (Ephesians 4:22–23). The only way your thoughts, views, and attitude will change is if you give your mind over to the Holy Spirit.

This starts with spending time in the Word of God, in prayer, and in meditation to understand what God says about your new way of life. What is God thinking? What is His thought process? How does He want you to start planning for your life? How does He want you to treat your neighbor, your spouse, your children? How does He want you to behave at work? How does He want you to take care of your health and invest your money, time, and talents?

You need to know what the Lord says, because you've been trying to do this on your own, and it's just not working out. When we accept Jesus Christ—His coming, His dying, and His rising on the third day—your culture changes from what you have planned for your life to what God has planned for your life.

> *"For I know the plans I have for you," declares the LORD, "plans to prosper you and not to harm you, plans to give you hope and a future."*
> **—Jeremiah 29:11**

You've seen where your own plans have gotten you and your family. The culture needs to change, and the only way it can is if you let the Holy Spirit come in and overhaul your way of thinking.

As Paul wrote, you need "to put on the new self, created to be like God in true righteousness and holiness" (Ephesians 4:24). You need to let go of your old self and allow God to transform you. You can't make yourself holy. God has the pattern of holiness. Only He knows how to get it done, so you must rely on Him to teach you how to overhaul and reshape your way of thinking.

When you lived in the old culture, your mind was dark. When you come to Christ, He shows you the reality of how deplorable and self-serving your life has been. Once He brings light to your mind, you have no business living in the old culture anymore.

Are you living to be miserable, to have your marriage on the rocks and your finances up in the air? Is your life as a Christian supposed to be chaos? No.

Overhaul the prisons of your life and come to an understanding of the love of Christ. It's because of His love and the blood He shed on Calvary that you no longer think like the world does.

If you no longer think like the world does, you should no longer live like the world does. You need a culture change. Ask Christ to reform your attitude and allow your new mindset to change your life. Then your new life will show the world that there is hope.

WORKBOOK

Chapter Two Questions

Question: What were some of the biggest changes that occurred in how you lived your life after you accepted Christ as your Savior? Are there other changes the Holy Spirit is leading you to make?

_____
_____
_____
_____
_____
_____
_____
_____
_____
_____

Question: Are there any situations in your life in which you are uncertain of God's perspective? Have you turned to God to seek His guidance? Have you read His Word to discover His views? If not, take some time to seek out God's heart in these matters.

_____
_____
_____
_____
_____
_____
_____
_____
_____
_____

Action: Create a chart with two columns. Title one column "Old Culture" and the other column "New Culture." In each column, list some characteristics of personal culture prior to Christ (old culture) and personal culture with Christ (new culture). Which column is more characteristic of your life? Does this reveal any changes you need to make to conform your life to the culture of Christ?

Chapter Two Notes

CHAPTER THREE

Charitable Giving

Read Matthew 6.

I like the closing of the year. In November, we begin to see how kind and thoughtful people can be. It seems as if the workers in any company become particularly friendly. There may be tragedies, but there are also people coming together to help others, regardless of color, gender, culture, and economic status.

People are so kind and thoughtful in November and December. Why can't this kindness exist outside of those months? There are ten months of the year when these acts are not even recognized. Kindness is put in a box somewhere. Are you waiting for November and December to show all of your kind acts?

We have organizations around the country that clothe people every single day. They beg for money to help people, but they don't get the same recognition in the news as those who do it in November and December.

Some folks won't even show up if the cameras aren't

there. Some great things may be going on around the country, and people who have influence won't do the daily work of consistent contribution. However, when the cameras arrive, they're the first people in the building. They're standing right in front of the reporters, telling them what the city is doing, when they haven't actually taken part in the charitable acts. If you do things to be seen by others, you will have no reward from God.

A Heart of Generosity

When we do things for people, we want somebody to know about it. We want recognition. We want to be seen as saviors on whom people can call in their time of need. Sometimes we want others to be indebted to us.

That's not the attitude of giving Jesus wants His followers to have. In Matthew 6, Jesus was talking about charitable giving. We can't mix up what society is asking of us with what God requires of us. Every year, we have 365 brand-new opportunities to do something for the Lord and to praise and honor Him in a way that brings Him glory.

Who Gets the Glory?

God set up charitable giving. When we have a heart like God's, it moves us to have compassion for all people. Even when we're down to our last piece of bread, we're still willing to give.

Jesus said, "When you give to the needy, do not let your left hand know what your right hand is doing"

(Matthew 6:3). In other words, don't announce what you are doing. The verses surrounding verse 3 contain the keyword *reward*; in the original, this is a word that means "to reward, recompense, render, whether in a good or bad sense."[2] Who gets the reward for our charitable giving? To whom is glory rendered for our fasting and praying?

The word *hypocrite* in verse 2 is referring to people who give to others for their own glory. They want the world to know the good things they do and honor them for their apparent generosity. As believers, we need to understand that the glory belongs to God. We're not in the position to be glorified or worshiped because of our charitable acts. God doesn't want us to do these things for ourselves, but for Him.

Be Careful of Motive

Jesus was giving instructions to those who choose to have a life like His. Don't be like the Pharisees, who blew the trumpet and wanted everyone to know the generous things they were doing. They wanted to be recognized, but Jesus was warning them to be careful. It's not enough to give. Motive matters.

We need to be careful to give with the desire to glorify God. If we are irritated or upset when the people we help don't show us appreciation, that's a sign that our motives are self-serving. If we want people to feel obligated to us when we give to them, we're not giving in the way Jesus taught us to give. We need to be careful not to engage in charitable acts for the sake of getting praise or anything else in return.

A Full Reward

Jesus said, "So when you give to the needy, do not announce it with trumpets, as the hypocrites do in the synagogues and on the streets, to be honored by others. Truly I tell you, they have received their reward in full" (Matthew 6:2).

Hypocrites want to be recognized in the streets and honored by the media. Instead of giving throughout the year, they wait for November and December to come around, when they know the cameras are out, looking for a good human-interest story. They may even be the ones who call in the tip and set it all up.

When people act out of self-righteousness and a desire for personal glory, they shouldn't look to heaven for a reward. There's no place in their spirit or attitude for the Lord's blessing because they've already received their blessing from men. They want to be recognized by men, so that's what they'll get.

God Will Recognize You

On the other hand, if you give in secret, "then your Father, who sees what is done in secret, will reward you" (Matthew 6:4). If you keep your ulterior motives out of it, then God will reward you. He may reward you secretly or openly. Either way, He knows that you will give Him the glory.

You need to stop worrying about other people recognizing you and start recognizing who your Father is. When you recognize who God is, you will have confidence that God will always reward a servant who is following His Word faithfully.

The Son of God walked on this earth for thirty-three and a half years, and He was falsely accused of blasphemy for saying that He was God in the flesh. They put a crown of thorns on His head and cursed Him. They beat Him and whipped Him, and they nailed Him to an old, rugged cross. He died on that cross and was buried, but on the third day, He rose to give us salvation. He sacrificed His life for us, and all He wants from those who serve Him is for us to give Him glory.

WORKBOOK

Chapter Three Questions

Question: Think of a time when you did something for someone else or provided something for someone else. Evaluate your motives honestly. Were you doing it for recognition from people, or was your heart set to please God?

_____
_____
_____
_____
_____
_____
_____
_____
_____

Question: How can you adjust your motives for generous living and align them with a desire to glorify God? Why is this important for a follower of Christ?

_____
_____
_____
_____
_____
_____
_____
_____

Action: Think of something generous you can do in secret, something no one but God will know about. Ask God to put a specific task on your heart. It can be something like sending money or a gift to someone you know is in need without letting the person know it's from you. Or perhaps you can find a charity with a Christ-centered mission and donate anonymously. How can you make anonymous giving a regular practice?

Chapter Three Notes

CHAPTER FOUR

Happy in God

Read Matthew 5:1–20.

The Sermon on the Mount was one of the first sermons Jesus gave during His time walking on the earth. When Jesus began to heal and deliver, folks began to follow Him everywhere He went. In this sermon, He preached to them about "beatitudes," or blessings.

The blessings Jesus shared with His followers were unusual. They weren't the kinds of blessings people normally thought of, like health and wealth. In fact, these blessings turned the world's version of happiness on its head.

In this sermon, Jesus had to change the disciples' attitude because they grew up in the world's way of thinking and motivating. Jesus set out to change their perception.

Your attitude will have to change, too. When your attitude changes, God can take you to high levels in every aspect of your life—in your marriage, your business, and your social relationships. The first four beatitudes Jesus mentioned capture the attitude change He wants for you. If you adopt these four perspectives, you will start seeing God at work in every circumstance of your life.

The Poor in Spirit: Change What's Inside

When we hear "poor in spirit" (Matthew 5:3), we may think of being destitute or being a beggar, but that's not what Jesus was talking about. He was teaching us that we have to change what's inside of us in order to change what's outside of us. It doesn't matter what the circumstances are on the outside. It's what you have on the inside that counts.

Things may not be going well, but does that change the way you praise? Is your praise determined by your circumstances, or do you give God your praise and gratitude in every situation?

Jesus said, "Apart from me you can do nothing" (John 15:5). To be "poor in spirit" means we acknowledge that without God, we can do nothing. We have bankrupted ourselves of the world's way of thinking and adapted to the Lord's way of thinking. When that change happens, "the new creation has come: The old has gone, the new is here!" (2 Corinthians 5:17).

When you gain this new attitude, it doesn't matter what happens to you on the outside. When the economy is in a recession, you're still grateful to the Lord. When your health is not good, you're still grateful to the Lord. When your job is on the rocks or you can't tell which way your business is going to go, you're still grateful to the Lord.

Romans 8:28 says, "And we know that in all things

God works for the good of those who love him, who have been called according to his purpose." It doesn't matter whether or not you like your circumstances. What matters is how you feel about God on the inside. When you have a great view of and attitude toward God, you can face anything in a godly way.

Do you remember when you used to give the bird to people who cut you off on the freeway (because you're a perfect driver and always innocent)? Maybe you even strung together some choice words. Now, since God has changed your attitude, when other vehicles jump in front of you, you can say, "Praise the Lord! Thank You for keeping me from an accident."

The Altar of God

When we're really frustrated with someone, we may be tempted to say, "You're on my last nerve!" However, there should be a place inside of us that we never allow anyone else to touch: the altar of our Savior. People can bug us, but we should never let them reach that place we reserve for the Holy Spirit. If we allow somebody to get to that spot, we have disavowed the Spirit and made someone else our god.

The Bible says, "In your anger do not sin" (Ephesians 4:26). When you allow someone else to control your actions, you're allowing outside circumstances to change the happiness inside. Jesus wants you to be happy in Him—not happy with money, not happy with honey, not happy with bunny.

People are looking for happiness in places where

happiness doesn't reside. Even if they find happiness, it's temporary. When the Bible says that "the joy of the LORD is your strength" (Nehemiah 8:10) but we look at everything else to bring us joy, we are living as if we consider God's words a lie. Job said, "Though he slay me, yet will I hope in him" (Job 13:15). We need to develop a trust in God that we don't allow the world to shake.

Because we are poor in spirit, we are new creatures. We can do nothing without Christ. If we trust that, then we are happy, for ours is the kingdom of heaven.

Those Who Mourn: Comfort Is Available

Jesus said, "Blessed are those who mourn, for they will be comforted" (Matthew 5:4). Have you ever had to mourn? If you're a parent, has there ever been a time when it was hard to put food on the table and the kids didn't know it? Maybe you broke down and cried. Be happy, even in that situation, because God has promised to bring you comfort.

Do you want to be of the world and keep mourning without comfort? If you're mourning, it may be challenging to transition to God's way of thinking. But if you do, you will find comfort.

Jesus understood that more than just His disciples were going to need comforting. God didn't want His disciples to have a monopoly on His comfort. He wants the whole world to feel His comfort.

The Word can comfort you when you're mourning. It won't just pat you on the back. There are times in life when we need an encouraging word from the Lord. We may need an encouraging word from Scripture or from the Holy Spirit.

A country song says, "Looking for love in all the wrong places, looking for love in empty spaces."[3] When the song ends, Johnny Lee was still looking for love! But God says, "When you accept me as Savior, your search is over. Nothing can transpire in your life that my Son hasn't already died for."

You will only receive God's comfort if you trust Him. If you don't trust the Word of God, then you can't depend on it to give you comfort. When you are mourning, you can be confident that you have a comforter, and His name is Jesus Christ.

Maybe you're concerned about your family, or maybe food isn't as readily available as it was last week, but you can still be happy in Jesus. Don't allow outside influences to press upon you so drastically that you can't praise God. Praise isn't determined by your circumstances. God wants us to be happy inside while He transforms us into rock-solid pillars of His love and truth on the earth.

The Meek: Be Grateful for God's Gifts

Jesus also said, "Blessed are the meek, for they will inherit the earth" (Matthew 5:5). Most people believe that it's important to be nice, kind, proper, and polite. We teach our children the basic principles of politeness: how to carry themselves in public and how to address adults as "sir" or "ma'am."

All of these things are good. However, the attitude of a believer should be even more respectful, compassionate, loving, and understanding. We can't get there without knowing who God is and how He asks us to behave. We have to investigate who God is, and He will show us what He expects of us. The meekness God wants from us is to be humble in spirit and to wait patiently on Him.

Psalm 37:11 says, "But the meek will inherit the land and enjoy peace and prosperity." When David wrote Psalm 37, he was an older man coming to the close of his life. He had seen some things that God had done and experienced God's deliverance, but he had also done things that brought a cloud over his family.

David was encouraging us not to be envious. Sometimes it may seem that others prosper easily. They know how to make money. They take advantage of the government and of people who are less educated. Some people even know that their time is limited, but they want all they can get now. God has a greater plan for us!

David was a humble shepherd boy. He was the youngest of his brothers. When the prophet came looking for him, he was out taking care of his sheep. That was his job.

Sometimes people who were once kind show a change of attitude after a little bit of education or a windfall. They become mean and arrogant. David was a nice, obedient young man, but he developed a different attitude when he became king. He did some things that were out of character.

Eventually, David was remorseful. His heart cried out to the Lord after the Bathsheba incident and when he saw the cloud of darkness over his family. Despite David's poor decisions, God held on to him because of the remorseful attitude he had.

David warned us about the jealousy of those who are prospering. Be meek, humble, and submissive to the Word of God. Don't have an arrogant attitude. Meekness says, "I'm grateful for what I have. If God gives me more, then praise Him!" Those who are aware that they need help are grateful for any blessing. They're mindful that their blessings come from above.

Galatians 3:18 says, "For if the inheritance depends on the law, then it no longer depends on the promise; but God in his grace gave it to Abraham through a promise." You might not have expected anything, but you have inherited something that will benefit not only you, but also your family for the rest of their lives.

We inherited the salvation of God. We didn't expect the healing power that came with it or the promises of God. We weren't expecting the joy, peace, purity, or compassion that came along with it. But God had all of this for us when we accepted Christ as our personal Savior. When you remain meek and humbly submissive to the Word of God, He will allow you to inherit the fruitful land of milk and honey.

Those Who Hunger and Thirst: Satisfaction in God's Word

In Matthew 5:6, Jesus said, "Blessed are those who hunger and thirst for righteousness, for they will be filled." Have you ever been hungry? I'm not just talking about being a little hungry. I'm talking about being famished. This isn't a case of not wanting what you have in the refrigerator. This is about having an empty stomach when there's nothing in the pantry, refrigerator, or microwave, and Mommy and Daddy are nowhere around. When you're starving, you're willing to eat almost anything. When you're thirsty, you need something to quench your thirst. Swallowing your saliva just won't work!

God says, "Happy are those who hunger and thirst for My righteousness as if there's nothing left in this world for them to eat or drink." You need to hunger for God as if there's a famine in the land and you know that there's some bread five miles away. Even if you have a spine problem and you're in a race with somebody faster, you're going to get that meal, no matter what!

Happy are those who desire the food of the Word of God. God always knows your voice when you cry out in thirst. He will feed you with courage, confidence, kindness, and a strong sense of gratefulness toward Him.

Perspective is a powerful thing. When you begin to see that God's blessings don't just come in the form of physical prosperity on this earth, you will walk with a peace that the world will notice. Allow God to shape your perspective so that you can see Him at work, no matter what you're going through in this life. Trusting Him in all things will bring unshakable peace to your heart.

A Heritage of Peace

With God, you can be happy when everything outside of you says that you ought to be depressed. We teach our kids, "Just be happy. Put on your smiley face." But it's not enough to put on a happy face. You need to have substance behind your happiness. If you don't, it's like trying to eat a baloney sandwich and then work an eight-hour shift. You need to put some beans and tortillas in your system. You need substance to give you energy.

God said that we're blessed, but sometimes we Christians are living like we lost the battle. Read the back of the Bible—we already won the victory! Then why are some Christians living defeated lives? Because they don't trust God. They let their outside circumstances weigh too heavily upon them. We can experience an attitude of happiness through God's blessings if we trust Him and His Word.

How is your attitude? Is it one of happiness in God? A God-honoring attitude always starts with meekness toward Him and obedience to His Word. There's evidence in the Bible of this. For example, Paul was once arrogant, but he changed his ways, and God blessed him. Was he a rich man? Yes, in Christ he was rich with joy, peace, and comfort.

Joy Beyond Understanding

When we have the right attitude and demonstrate godly character, we will experience a joy that surpasses the world's understanding. The world will wonder how we can rejoice in God when our house is up for foreclosure, our grandchildren are living in conditions that trouble our hearts, or we have a funeral for our mother. How can we be joyful in times of trouble? Because God has given us an inheritance not only of salvation and prosperity, but also of peace.

Those who follow God's commands delight in Him.

Delight yourself in the Lord and in His Word. Then He "will give you the desires of your heart" (Psalm 37:4).

Peace Beyond Understanding

We can find comfort in all that God has given us. There will be some cloudy and stormy times in our lives, but they won't last forever. We will endure through the night, and joy will come in the morning (Psalm 30:5).

If we believe and trust in the Word of God, we can understand that we are inheriting the grace, mercy, and peace God has for us. We can also delight in what we don't understand.

The world gives you a light-switch peace. You turn it on, and it's bright and cool. But in the heat of the day, you have to turn it off. Why? Because it gets too hot. God gives us a different kind of peace.

Jesus said, "I have told you these things, so that in me you may have peace. In this world you will have trouble. But take heart! I have overcome the world" (John 16:33). God never guaranteed us a trouble-free life. In fact, He said that we would definitely have trouble! How, then, can we have peace? Because we know that God has overcome everything that can and will press upon us.

No matter what's going on, God already has the victory. Since we're in Christ, the tribulations of this world won't overtake us. When we have the inheritance of God and a godly attitude, God will take care of everything that surrounds us. Knowing that gives us peace.

Colossians 3:15 says, "Let the peace of Christ rule in your hearts, since as members of one body you were called to peace. And be thankful." If you entrust all of your cares to God, "the peace of God, which transcends all understanding, will guard your hearts and your minds in Christ Jesus" (Philippians 4:7).

Some of the things God has done in my life I don't even understand, and I don't think I'm the only one. But God's peace goes beyond our understanding. It's not limited to our logic, and it will guard our hearts and minds to keep us secure and help us to make the right decisions when the circumstances in our lives threaten to overwhelm us. Even if a situation looks bad, God is at work. He is aware of what's going on, and He won't leave us to deal with it alone.

WORKBOOK

Chapter Four Questions

Question: When you received Christ, what were some of the unexpected benefits you experienced as a result of your salvation?

_____

_____

_____

_____

_____

_____

_____

_____

_____

_____

Question: How do your circumstances affect your mood? Is your attitude easily dictated by your situation? On what truths can you focus to sustain a perspective of joy and peace even in the midst of challenging situations?

_____

_____

_____

_____

_____

_____

_____

_____

_____

_____

Action: Memorize Colossians 3:15 and Philippians 4:7. When facing external circumstances that attempt to distract you from the peace of God, meditate on these verses.

Chapter Four Notes

CHAPTER FIVE

A Reason for Praise

Read Philippians 4.

My sister-in-law is currently going through chemo. She wakes up strong every morning and has peace with it, but my brother is struggling. Our mothers are aging, and sometimes we go overboard trying to care for them (but they put us back in our places).

Through all of these things—the heartache, the depression, and the stress—there has to be something that gets us out of the funk. When it seems like our lives and the whole world are barreling downhill, and we have no way to put on the brakes, there's still a reason to praise God. There's a reason in light of all that we're going through to praise the living God.

When Paul wrote to the Philippians, the church was being persecuted. Ever since Jesus had been crucified, His followers had faced mistreatment that, I'm sure, challenged them to hold on to their faith. In our lifetime, we may not have people threatening our lives for worshiping

God, but we all have gone through some kind of heartache or heartbreak. These struggles might have pulled us temporarily away from God to look at the challenge before us. Paul was telling the Philippians, as well as Christians today, to move away from those things of the flesh. Don't allow yourself to be influenced by what Christ has delivered you from.

You Can't Stop Living

When challenges come our way, we can't just stop living, serving, and trusting. Based on Paul's mention of "chains" (Philippians 1:7, 13) and facing the possibility of death (Philippians 1:18–26), we know that he was locked up when he wrote this letter, no doubt for preaching the gospel. Paul was saying, "I'm in jail. You're free. I know you're having issues, but I'm telling you that God is worthy of your praise."

Don't Allow Tears to Cloud Your Vision

There's a reason we go through things in life: to strengthen our faith. We can't see that when we're going through a difficult or painful time, because our vision is clouded by our tears.

Have you ever been driving when rain was coming down so hard that the windshield wipers were ineffective? Maybe you couldn't see anything in front of you, so you pulled over because it was unsafe to continue. As Christians, it's unsafe for us to continue allowing our tears to flood our vision, because then we can't see the growth that

God is accomplishing in us.

While Paul was in jail, he wasn't moaning about his situation. Instead, he was encouraging others in the faith. You might have lost someone you love, your marriage may be on the rocks, or your finances may be about to drop, but you can encourage someone else.

Paul wrote, "Let your gentleness be evident to all. The Lord is near" (Philippians 4:5). You may be grieving and hurting, but you need to let the world know that the Lord Jesus hasn't forgotten about you. Open your heart and sing praises to the Lord.

There are opportunities we miss because we allow tears to flood our eyes. We don't want to say anything to anybody, because we're so consumed by our own grief. You do need to grieve, but don't let that stop your praise. Take the opportunity to witness for the Lord, and it will help with your grieving.

God Is in Control

> *Do not be anxious about anything, but in every situation, by prayer and petition, with thanksgiving, present your requests to God.*
> ***—Philippians 4:6***

God is in control. His hand is upon everything that's happening. You may be confused and bewildered, but God is not.

When we know without a shadow of a doubt that God is in control, that will certainly bring us some comfort. He knows about our problems. He knows about our hurt, suffering, and loneliness.

We serve a God who is holding our hands. The same God who holds our hands through loss, tragedy, and grieving will hold our hands as He leads us to His eternal glory. Sometimes we get so deep, dark, and depressed that we forget that we still have a reason to praise. In all of our challenges, where is God? He is right there with us.

Think About These Things

A faith that isn't tested can't be trusted. What's true about your tragedy? God is real. He controls all, and He knows your situation. God is still worthy of your praise when you are hurting, because He will walk with you through your struggles.

It takes faith to praise God in hard times. Whether you're having trouble with your health, your family, or your finances, you need to have faith that God can and will take care of you. Say, "I'm tired of hanging my head. I want to feel Your joy again."

It brings me tremendous comfort in the midst of a heartbreaking or disturbing situation to recognize that God allowed it. Then I can be open to the lesson God wants me to learn from that struggle or heartache. Instead of asking, "God, why is this happening to me?" I should be asking, "God, what are You trying to show me?"

I am confident that God is good, and He doesn't allow anything to come into our lives to destroy us when we are trusting Him. Ultimately, He allows things to bring a blessing or a lesson—oftentimes both.

WORKBOOK

Chapter Five Questions

Question: Are you finding it difficult to praise God in your current circumstances? How is that affecting your relationship with Him?

_____
_____
_____
_____
_____
_____
_____
_____
_____
_____
_____

Question: Why do you think it's hard to praise God when your life is difficult, painful, or lonely? How and why do challenging circumstances distract you from the goodness of God?

_____
_____
_____
_____
_____
_____
_____
_____
_____
_____

Action: Find a worship song that exalts the nature and heart of God. Go to a quiet place where you can be alone and focus on God without distractions. Allow the truth of the song of praise to fill your mind and heart. Continue worshiping until you feel a shift in your mindset.

Chapter Five Notes

CHAPTER SIX

The God of the Impossible

Read 2 Kings 5:1–14.

When there's something wrong in our lives, we want it to come to an end. None of us like struggling or being sick all day, every day. We want the pain to subside. We want relief from the pressure. We want our economy to get back in line. We want the recession to end. There are things in this world that we are waiting on God to bring to an end. There's no worse feeling than being stuck. That emotion alone can cause a deep, dark depression.

Have you ever had a testimony after going through something difficult and seeing God work in that situation? Everyone's struggle has to have an ending, and it was no different for Naaman.

Waiting on God

Have you ever waited on something? Maybe you're waiting on the debates in your relationship to be resolved.

Maybe you're waiting on your children to wake up. Maybe you're waiting on a job promotion. Maybe you're waiting on your government or community to straighten out. We find ourselves waiting a lot. We're waiting for something to happen.

> *Now Naaman was commander of the army of the king of Aram. He was a great man in the sight of his master and highly regarded, because through him the LORD had given victory to Aram. He was a valiant soldier, but he had leprosy.*
>
> **—2 Kings 5:1**

Can you imagine this victorious man of God? This man had favor upon his life. As a commander, he had people under him. He had the favor of the king and the favor of God. After all those battles he was in, getting a nick here and there but surviving, now he was faced with certain death. Who could deliver him?

He was the commander of the king of Aram's army, but then he got sick. The Bible doesn't tell us how he got leprosy, but at this particular time in history, there was no cure. He was just waiting to die.

However, Naaman didn't want the obvious ending. He wanted a different ending, but he didn't know where to go. He was encouraged to look to God.

The Impossible

Once a lady in my congregation had an aneurysm. Before this, I only knew of people who died from aneurysms.

However, this woman lived! Her speech was slurred, but she was living. I couldn't believe it. God gave her a different conclusion to the story, and she had a testimony to share.

We serve a God of the impossible. He can do anything. God is the God of all cures. He can open all doors because He has the power and authority. The end of a struggle leads to a testimony that reveals an impossible thing God has done.

In the story of Naaman, a young girl said that there was a prophet in Samaria who could heal Naaman:

> *Naaman went to his master and told him what the girl from Israel had said. "By all means, go," the king of Aram replied. "I will send a letter to the king of Israel." So Naaman left, taking with him ten talents of silver, six thousand shekels of gold and ten sets of clothing.*
> —*2 Kings 5:4–5*

There's nothing in the text to indicate that the king questioned Naaman at all. He could have asked where the young girl was from and where she had gotten her information. However, those questions would have delayed the blessing God had for Naaman.

A Misprint

> *The letter that he took to the king of Israel read: "With this letter I am sending my servant Naaman to you so that you may cure him of his leprosy."*
> —*2 Kings 5:6*

I think that was something of a misprint. The king wasn't expected to do the healing personally, but the healing fell within the king's providence.

> *As soon as the king of Israel read the letter, he tore his robes and said, "Am I God? Can I kill and bring back to life? Why does this fellow send someone to me to be cured of his leprosy? See how he is trying to pick a quarrel with me!"*
> —**2 Kings 5:7**

It's not like Naaman stubbed his toe. He came to the king with an incurable, deadly disease. The king read the letter right, but the letter was wrong.

Have you ever said something that was received wrong? Maybe the wording of it wasn't right, and the other person misunderstood your intention. The wording of this letter must not have been correct, because the king responded, "Are you trying to insult me? Did you really send me all of these gifts on top of the insult? Are you trying to make me think that I'm a god?"

The king knew that he didn't have the authority to heal Naaman. Some preachers these days put their hands on people to heal them, quacking like chickens and flapping their arms like wings. You may think that you need to go to them to be healed, but you need to go to God.

My sister-in-law once said, "These things were designed to make us pray." The struggle was designed to help you to put your trust back where it belongs: in God. Your testimony can't end with worldly things. It has to end with the blessing of the living God.

The king of Israel knew that Naaman was a

commander. He wasn't ignorant. He might not have had Instagram or Facebook, but he knew. It's wonderful how God brings to the people of God the things they need to hear.

> *When Elisha the man of God heard that the king of Israel had torn his robes, he sent him this message: "Why have you torn your robes? Have the man come to me and he will know that there is a prophet in Israel."*
> —**2 Kings 5:8**

God can resurrect your relationships. He can restore your livelihood. When you're down to your last breath, God can give you another one. He can turn your community around. Then you'll have a testimony of the goodness, favor, and love of the living God.

Pride vs. Obedience

> *So Naaman went with his horses and chariots and stopped at the door of Elisha's house. Elisha sent a messenger to say to him, "Go, wash yourself seven times in the Jordan, and your flesh will be restored and you will be cleansed."*
> —**2 Kings 5:9-10**

Because of Naaman's position, he had a little pride. Elisha sent him a message but didn't come to the door. On top of that, the Jordan wasn't the cleanest of rivers. Naaman took issue with all of this:

> *But Naaman went away angry and said, "I thought that he would surely come out to me and stand and call on the name of the LORD his God, wave his hand over the spot and cure me of my leprosy."*
> —**2 Kings 5:11**

Sometimes you don't simply want God to fix your problem. In your pride, you want Him to do it your way. You just use God as a prop. You want to get out of your situation, so you pray to God just to get it done. Then God doesn't do it your way, and you get frustrated.

Naaman thought, "I'm too important for him to send a message to me. Doesn't he know that I command thousands of men? My authority gives me the right to a face-to-face consultation and a hands-on healing, but this guy has the audacity to send me a message! Doesn't he know how far I've come?"

Naaman lost his mind a little bit. Maybe he forgot what a prophet was. Maybe he forgot that this prophet was inspired and sent by God. Maybe he forgot the power he felt when he first heard about the prophet in Samaria. Maybe he forgot the long journey and all the gold he had brought.

Pride is an ugly thing. Pride will keep you from God's blessing. If you are blessed, your family will be blessed. If your family is blessed, your nation will be blessed. If we have pride in the White House, our nation is cursed.

Naaman continued his rant: "Are not Abana and Pharpar, the rivers of Damascus, better than all the waters of Israel? Couldn't I wash in them and be cleansed?" (2 Kings 5:12). He was saying, "I know some cleaner rivers, bro! Aren't those two rivers better?" But sometimes a cleaner river won't get the job done. Sometimes a little dirt can help you.

When God calls for humility, pride raises its ugly head. There are some things that can be fixed by agencies in our world, but because of pride, people are dying.

Sometimes the simple stuff makes sense. Not only did Naaman's wife love him, but his servants loved him, too. They said to Naaman, "My father, if the prophet had told you to do some great thing, would you not have done it? How much more, then, when he tells you, 'Wash and be cleansed'!" (2 Kings 5:13).

Sometimes I make things too complicated, and I think of my wife, who makes things simple. She simplifies my most complicated sayings. She can say in five words what I say in ten, and she still gets the same point across. I love that about her.

The servants were saying, "Boss man, we know that you're hurting. We came all this way for you to be healed. We know, your wife knows, and the king of Aram knows that what you have is going to kill you. There's no cure, and your pride is keeping you from the chance to be healed. If you do what this prophet says, it won't kill you, but this disease definitely will kill you, so at least give it a try." The servants displayed the love and humility that was necessary—that Naaman should have had but didn't.

Do you go to church to be healed? Do you go to God to be healed? Are you there with a humble heart because you need healing, or are you there because you're obligated to be there and you think that God owes you?

A Transformed Life

> *So he went down and dipped himself in the Jordan seven times, as the man of God had told him, and his flesh was restored and became clean like that of a young boy.*
> —**2 Kings 5:14**

Naaman did what the man of God instructed him to do, and he was healed of his incurable disease.

When you receive Christ as your Savior, the Bible says, "Behold, all things have become new" (2 Corinthians 5:17 NKJV). Your life is transformed. You're about to embark on a journey led by the Word of God, the Spirit of God, the navigation and direction of God, and your life will never be the same again.

When you let go of your pride in fighting for your marriage or your financial situation and start trusting God, your mind will be at peace. Dip yourself seven times. Ask God to work on you, and do what He says.

How beautiful it is to say, "I remember when I was going through that terrible time. I thought that I was losing my mind. My marriage was crumbling, and I didn't know what to do. I felt helpless, like I was being trampled. But the Spirit of God came to me when I prayed, and God gave me a word that touched my heart: my struggle would end. Today I have a testimony. Weeping only lasts for a night, and joy comes in the morning."

WORKBOOK

Chapter Six Questions

Question: Describe a time when you were waiting on God and He came through for you. What did you learn about God's character through that experience?

_____

_____

_____

_____

_____

_____

_____

_____

_____

Question: When you go to God in prayer, do you truly seek His will, or do you want God to bend to your agenda? How can you distinguish between your personal desires and what God wants for you?

_____
_____
_____
_____
_____
_____
_____
_____
_____
_____

Action: In a notebook, journal, or computer document, record the faithfulness of God in your life. Write down all the times in your life when God came through for you. Continue to add to this list any time God shows Himself faithful in your life. When you encounter difficult times, refer to this record and remind yourself of God's unchanging nature.

Chapter Six Notes

CHAPTER SEVEN

Faith in Life's Battles

Read 1 Samuel 17.

Life is full of change, and sometimes those changing circumstances lead us into battles. Sometimes we anticipate the changes that will occur, and sometimes we don't. David didn't know what would happen when he brought his brothers some food per his father's instructions. He wasn't going there to fight, just to deliver food. When he got there, he met Goliath, the giant Philistine.

Today your enemy could be a person, a situation, or an addiction. How did you get there? And once you get there, what's your process to develop and to adapt to the particular change? When something interferes with the normal progression of life, you need to figure out how you're going to handle it—physically, mentally, and spiritually.

Fighting Against Experience

Twice a day, Goliath would challenge the army of Israel to send forth a man to fight him (1 Samuel 17:8–10, 16). Some people would get tired of hearing that speech, but the army of Israel was afraid. Goliath was about nine feet tall and an experienced warrior. He'd been trained in warfare from his youth (1 Samuel 17:33).

In a lot of the battles we face, we're fighting against experience. Addiction has experience in enslaving lives. Disappointment has experience in keeping you down. Defiance has experience in capturing your attention span, your time, and your energy.

Too often we think that we're not good enough because we lack education or whatever other qualification we think would make us worthy to take on a particular challenge or calling. But we can fight against this when we realize that in the body of Christ, qualifications come from the Holy Spirit. God *will* qualify you for any mission He sends you on, whether or not you've been to seminary or have the "right" experience listed on your résumé.

When I was writing this manuscript, I knew that I needed assistance. I didn't have the experience, but I was aided by someone who did. God gave me a calling, and He provided a way for me to rise to the challenge of a situation I didn't feel qualified to handle. On whom are you going to depend when you face a battle against experience?

Fighting Against Procrastination

The Israelites really wanted this Philistine killed. They saw each other every day. Goliath was the only one coming out, even though he had an army behind him. The Israelites stood there every day, facing the Philistines, and they camped right across the valley. But no one would fight Goliath. I guess they thought, "One day, I'm going to overcome my fear and fight. Or maybe the other army will just go home."

Why are we constantly waiting to fight? Sometimes we know why we need to fight a battle, but we're hesitant to do what needs to be done. Why are we constantly looking at what we fear and accepting the defeat instead of doing something about it?

Procrastination kills us in a spiritual battle. This happens when we hesitate when God tells us to move or react to a challenge. We get in the way of God when He has already made the way for us.

I remember when I was pastoring Miracle Temple Mission Church in Dallas in 2001. I honestly felt like I didn't deserve that position. I had procrastinated in listening to God's call upon my life for so long. I knew that God had called me to preach, but I hesitated. However, He changed my heart to care for His people.

Procrastination gets obliterated when God lights your heart on fire for His cause. God surrounded me with praying and encouraging saints and broke through my desire to procrastinate. God is also working His plan through you for His glory, so don't wait any longer. When He speaks, move!

Fighting Against Defiance

> *David asked the men standing near him, "What will be done for the man who kills this Philistine and removes this disgrace from Israel? Who is this uncircumcised Philistine that he should defy the armies of the living God?"*
> —*1 Samuel 17:26*

David might have thought, "Am I really hearing this?" Surely there was somebody in the Israelite army who had been practicing warfare for a long time and could compete with Goliath. David was saying, "This person we are afraid of defies the God we serve!" When we go through challenges, we have a way of relying on ourselves or other people to help us. Then, when everything else fails, we come back to place our trust in God.

Fighting Against Fear

> *When Eliab, David's oldest brother, heard him speaking with the men, he burned with anger at him and asked, "Why have you come down here? And with whom did you leave those few sheep in the wilderness? I know how conceited you are and how wicked your heart is; you came down only to watch the battle."*
> —*1 Samuel 17:28*

The older brother knew that David had come to bring food, but he didn't want his little brother to see how afraid he was. He called David conceited and uppity. He insulted his brother in front of other men, but that was his fear talking.

When we face battles, sometimes we don't want others to know how afraid we are. But hiding it won't help, and lashing out won't help. There comes a time when we need to call upon the living God. David was a determined man who believed in God's power.

Don't Lose Heart

David was a shepherd, not a fighter. He was the youngest of his father's sons. Even though he was small compared to Goliath, there was something bold enough in David to say, "Don't lose heart!" David didn't depend on his size, his strength, or his skills. He depended on the Lord.

Don't let the fear of this world do the talking in your heart. Depend on the Lord. Are you going to give in to the world, or do you believe God when He says that He is with you?

God's Deliverance

We need to get a faith app that shows us when God delivered us from heartache, depression, or sickness. Wouldn't that be great? It would remind us of when God helped us before so we could say, "I believe that the same God can deliver me now."

David's Résumé

David said, "It doesn't matter to me what weapons I have or the power and strength Goliath possesses. I won't lose heart!" It doesn't matter what the doctor says, what the bank says, or what the world says. What matters is that you know God is with you and will fight for you.

In your own power, you can't win. In your own strength, the changes of life will defeat you. You have no recourse. But when you're with the Lord, He is your "refuge and strength, an ever-present help in trouble" (Psalm 46:1).

David gave Saul his résumé. He let Saul know why fear wasn't in his heart (1 Samuel 17:34–37). Like David, when we put our trust in the Lord, we can face any odds without fear.

Charging the Enemy

When Goliath saw David, "he looked David over and saw that he was little more than a boy, glowing with health and handsome, and he despised him" (1 Samuel 17:42). Because of David's size and inexperience, Goliath was insulted that David would even come up to him and talk to him, let alone try to fight him.

When the enemy is coming at you, you have to charge at him with the power of God. With His power, David released the slingshot. Goliath fell facedown, and David cut off his head (1 Samuel 17:48–51). The rest of the Israelite army chased the Philistines and killed them (1 Samuel 17:52).

David had no idea that he would be fighting that day when all he was doing was carrying food to his older brothers. David had no idea that fighting a lion and a bear to protect his father's sheep was preparing him to face a giant warrior on the battlefield. David didn't know that trusting God for those things would teach him to trust God for other things.

You don't know what battles the future holds, so use every opportunity to strengthen your trust in God. Build an anthem of faith so that when the battles come, you'll know that you can depend on the Lord and face your enemies without fear.

WORKBOOK

Chapter Seven Questions

Question: What battles do you face right now in your life? What Goliaths are standing before you today?

_____
_____
_____
_____
_____
_____
_____
_____
_____
_____
_____

Question: What tools has God provided for you to help you fight your battles? How can you be successful in overcoming your struggles, temptations, sin patterns, and addictions?

_____
_____
_____
_____
_____
_____
_____
_____
_____
_____

Action: Create an anthem or declaration of faith. It doesn't have to be musical, but write out something that expresses your faith in God and your reasons for that faith. For example, list the different attributes of God and the circumstances in which you have experienced God's faithfulness. Reflect on this anthem any time you encounter battles in your life.

Chapter Seven Notes

CHAPTER EIGHT

God's Power Against Our Sin

Read Exodus 14.

The Israelites had been in Egypt for 430 years (Exodus 12:40–41). They were enslaved, but God delivered them out of Egypt (Exodus 12). They went into Egypt with seventy people (Exodus 1:5), and when God delivered them, they came out of Egypt with 600,000 men, plus women and children (Exodus 12:37). When God said that it was time for the Israelites to leave Egypt, Pharaoh wouldn't let them go (Exodus 7–10). When he finally did let them go, he pursued them (Exodus 14:5–9).

When you repent of sin, it will still try to pursue you. It will come back in some form and try to recapture you. Sin doesn't want to let you go like Pharaoh wouldn't let the Israelites go.

Sin Wants You Back

Sin is always determined to get you back. If you leave a crack in the door, sin will come through. You may think that it's over, that sin has forgotten about you, but it's not over. If you don't keep watching, fighting, and praying, sin will creep back through the door. It may slip past your door through your kids. Do you see the traits in your children? Or maybe they don't affect you, but your grandchildren do.

You'd think that after all the plagues that fell upon Egypt, Pharaoh would have wanted nothing more to do with the Israelites. You'd think that the blood, the frogs, the locusts, and the death of the firstborn would have been enough, but sin is stubborn.

> *When the king of Egypt was told that the people had fled, Pharaoh and his officials changed their minds about them and said, "What have we done? We have let the Israelites go and have lost their services!"*
> *—Exodus 14:5*

Similarly, when we are delivered from sin, Satan has lost our service. I don't know about you, but I was a good servant. I was there every Friday. I was determined to do what I wanted to do. When God came into my life and the Spirit of God brought me out of that world and into His glory, my mind and heart began to change.

When your heart and mind begin to change from Satan's desires to God's desires, Satan doesn't forget what you like. He knows that if he can get you to do one simple act, he's got you back in his grasp.

Pharaoh wanted his slaves back so badly that every chariot employed in Egypt was sent after the Israelites. Pharaoh used every resource he had to go after the children of Israel.

> The Egyptians—all Pharaoh's horses and chariots, horsemen and troops—pursued the Israelites and overtook them as they camped by the sea near Pi Hahiroth, opposite Baal Zephon.
> —*Exodus 14:9*

When sin sees that you won't come back on your own, not only will it come after you, but it'll send others along with it to make sure that you come back.

We're never far from sin. Some of us believe that we're all right, that we can handle it now. We've been away from it for three, four, five years. As soon as we start to think that way, sin has a way back into our hearts and lives. What do we do when it shows up again?

A Rock and a Hard Place

When Pharaoh and his army came after the Israelites, the people of Israel were stuck between a rock and a hard place. On both sides of them were mountains, and in front of them was the Red Sea. Pharaoh and his homeboys were coming up fast behind them. They were trapped.

Sometimes when God stands up for us, it's not to make us bolder in the face of the world, but to show the world and us that there's no power greater than His. Sometimes

God will place us in an adverse situation just to display His glory! When God delivers you out of something, it's important to remember what He did. God was preparing the children of Israel to declare His glory and power.

Israel was held up in a valley, and there were walls on both sides. Dr. Maurice Ricks, pastor of Sure Foundation Baptist Church, once said it this way: "They were in a cul-de-sac, and there was only one way out." God placed them there, and there was nowhere else to turn. Sometimes we feel trapped, but we need to watch and wait patiently for what God is going to do.

Uncertainty and Fear

When fear comes, uncertainty follows. Sometimes we have a feeling of what God will do, but because the world tells us that we must do something for ourselves, we feel unsure. Our faith falters, and we worry about things we shouldn't be worried about. Satan wants us to be unsure of what God will do in our lives.

So what did God do when the Israelites were trapped? He just let them stew. Sometimes we want God to come, but He is already there. We're just too worked up with fear and worry to see Him. We already know that there's nothing we can do to prevent what's going to come upon us. If we could have stopped ourselves from sinning, we wouldn't need God. God has come into our lives to change us by His own power. All we need to do is trust Him and watch Him work.

Trusting God's Plan

> As Pharaoh approached, the Israelites looked up, and there were the Egyptians, marching after them. They were terrified and cried out to the LORD. They said to Moses, "Was it because there were no graves in Egypt that you brought us to the desert to die? What have you done to us by bringing us out of Egypt? Didn't we say to you in Egypt, 'Leave us alone; let us serve the Egyptians'? It would have been better for us to serve the Egyptians than to die in the desert!"
>
> —*Exodus 14:10-12*

The Israelites quickly forgot how God had delivered them from slavery. We, too, can be so busy looking back on our old life of sin that we don't see the power of God at work to do new things in our lives. The world is looking for the hope we have, but how can we share it if we're looking back, believing the lie that we had it better when we were slaves to sin?

How could the Israelites try to discredit God's deliverer for bringing them away from watching their mothers, sisters, and children be raped? How could they think that was okay? How can you say that seeing your family stuck on alcohol or drugs or living in prostitution is all right with you? Is shooting and killing in our schools okay?

The Israelites weren't complaining before they saw the enemy. They weren't complaining as long as God was in front of them and they could see His provision. But as soon as they saw the enemy coming, they panicked because they couldn't see a way out of the situation themselves.

We do the same thing when we depend on the world instead of God. When we do that, we're on our way to hell. Kingdom-minded folks don't see what the world sees, because faith doesn't work like that. Kingdom-minded folks understand that faith is a substance. They know that what they see in God is more than what they can see with their human eyes. In time, God will show them glory that hasn't yet been revealed.

When you give yourself to Kingdom work, God will elevate you and promote you, whether you want it or not. God's promises come to pass. You may be terrified when you see sin pursuing you, but 1 Corinthians 10:13 tells us that sin is not a new thing: "No temptation has overtaken you except what is common to mankind." God will faithfully supply an escape for you, and when you see it, take it! Your reaction to sin should be to repent, and then God will forgive you and clear your conscience (1 John 1:9).

God is looking to make a dramatic difference in your life. He wants to do something new. Don't deny the transformation out of fear of the unfamiliar or because of the crowd you hang out with. Turn to God and allow Him to purify you from the inside out.

WORKBOOK

Chapter Eight Questions

Question: Is there a sin in your life that you struggle to overcome, a sin that keeps circling back around and meeting you face to face? Why is that sin a stumbling block for you?

_____
_____
_____
_____
_____
_____
_____
_____
_____
_____

Question: What has God done for you to help you overcome sin? How should you respond when you face sin or feel trapped by it?

_____
_____
_____
_____
_____
_____
_____
_____
_____

Action: Is there any sin in your life of which you need to repent? Take some time in God's presence. Confess your sin to God. Allow His forgiveness to wash over you and clear your conscience.

Chapter Eight Notes

CHAPTER NINE

Resurrecting the Dead

Read John 11:1–44.

The dead need to be revived—dead marriages, children, and decisions that we make. Once we give our lives to Jesus, we may try to sit on the bench to get out of the game of life, but instead our gifts need to be reshaped. God can use a gift that you had in the world to glorify Him instead.

When Jesus heard that Lazarus was sick, He said, "This sickness will not end in death. No, it is for God's glory so that God's Son may be glorified through it" (John 11:4). Some of our sickness and hard times won't conclude in death; they are for God's glory. We have tough issues in our lives, marriages, health, and finances, but when we depend on God, He works everything out for His glory. When He works out our difficulties according to His will, it grows His saints.

Witnesses to His Glory

> *After he had said this, he went on to tell them, "Our friend Lazarus has fallen asleep; but I am going there to wake him up."*
>
> *His disciples replied, "Lord, if he sleeps, he will get better." Jesus had been speaking of his death, but his disciples thought he meant natural sleep.*
>
> *So then he told them plainly, "Lazarus is dead, and for your sake I am glad I was not there, so that you may believe. But let us go to him."*
> —*John 11:11-14*

Sometimes Jesus needs to correct our thinking. Lazarus wasn't asleep; he was dead—in the world's eyes. If we look at it from our worldly view, Lazarus had departed from the land of the living. He was no longer among them in his natural state. He was dead.

Jesus knew that His disciples' faith would be increased by what was about to happen with Lazarus. They would need that faith when Jesus died. He wouldn't always be with His disciples in His physical state. They would need to believe that even in His physical absence, He was alive and truly the Messiah.

What God Already Gave Us

Even when we know that God has brought us through difficult times in the past and solved problems for us, we may still question Him when the next challenge comes along. We may ask, "God, where are You? I've been faithful to You, and I know that You have been with me in the past, but now I can't hear You. I can't see Your hand moving in my life." We need to trust God even when we can't trace it.

In the Ray Charles movie, he lost his sight when he was a little boy. He was coming into the house, feeling his way, and he fell to the floor. His mother made a move to go after him, and she caught herself. He said, "Mama, where are you? I need you!"[4]

Sometimes we get into trouble and call out to God, "Where are You? I need You!" But God is already there. When we understand that He is with us, we can begin to move forward.

Ray heard a cricket and the wood crackling in the fireplace. He began to move toward the cricket because he realized that he had some senses that weren't dead. His sight might have been dead, but his hearing wasn't dead.

Your feelings may be dead, but your relationship isn't. The Holy Spirit is still alive in you. Use what you have. Sometimes we look for God to do something miraculous, but He has already done the work that He needs to do in us. We need to recall that work and let it carry us through the next challenge.

Wait on God

When Jesus arrived on the scene, He "found that Lazarus had already been in the tomb for four days" (John 11:17). This is an important detail because it shows the lack of hope there was for a healing or a resurrection. If the body was in the ground for four days, there was no hope for that person to come to life again. The decaying of skin had already begun, and the worms had started to make their way in. There was no hope for the body.

Sometimes we think that there's no more hope for our marriages, health, finances, decision-making, or education, but God says, "As long as you trust Me and you have breath in your body, don't dare think that I can't revive you." God can revive those dead things. Not only did Jesus know the Word of God, because He was the Word, but He also knew the traditions of man and wanted to show the glory of His Father, that we may believe all the more.

Mary, Lazarus's sister, fell at Jesus' feet and said, "Lord, if you had been here, my brother would not have died" (John 11:32). Mary had faith up to a point, but she failed to see that trusting in Jesus means trusting in His timing and believing that He has the power to deal with impossible situations. Where the world sees no hope, in Jesus there is hope.

If we had waited for Jesus, we wouldn't be dead in our employment. We wouldn't be dead in our marriages. We wouldn't be dead in our relationships. If we had held on and trusted God instead of letting our minds overrun our confidence in Him, we would have defeated death.

Powerful Truth

Jesus said to Martha, Lazarus's other sister, "I am the resurrection and the life. The one who believes in me will live, even though they die; and whoever lives by believing in me will never die. Do you believe this?" (John 11:25–26).

When you receive truth, the Spirit of God in you recognizes the truth. When you recognize truth, there's really nothing more you can say, because the truth has already said it for you. It's time to act according to what the truth has made clear to you. Once you know the truth, "the truth will set you free" (John 8:32).

> *"Yes, Lord," she replied, "I believe that you are the Messiah, the Son of God, who is to come into the world."*
>
> *After she had said this, she went back and called her sister Mary aside. "The Teacher is here," she said, "and is asking for you."*
>
> *—John 11:27–28*

Why do you call on God? Why do you call on the resurrected Lord, who bled and died and was laid in a borrowed tomb? Why do you call on the One who was raised out of the tomb on the third day? You call on Him because you know that He is the Son of God, but do you also know that He is the resurrection? Those who believe in Jesus Christ never die. Even if they leave this world, they never really die, because they are part of God's eternal kingdom.

> *When Jesus saw her weeping, and the Jews who had come along with her also weeping, he was deeply moved in spirit and troubled. "Where have you laid him?" he asked.*
>
> *"Come and see, Lord," they replied.*
>
> *Jesus wept.*
>
> *—John 11:33–35*

There's a lot of speculation about why Jesus wept. It's a challenge for me to see that Jesus became so emotional in the human form. Is it possible that this weeping was for the disbelief around Him?

Some people cry when they feel hopeless. When you've done all you can do and tried all you can try but there's no help anywhere, wouldn't you cry? That's just being human.

But Jesus was focused on what God wanted. He knew that He could revive what was dead. Then God would be glorified, and faith, trust, and belief in His Son would increase for all who witnessed the miracle. They would be able to tell the world that Lazarus was once dead, but in Jesus there's life forevermore.

Your relationship doesn't have to be dead. God can revive it. Your emotions don't have to be dead. God can revive them. We must believe that God can do the impossible—and give glory to Him when He does.

These people who stood at the tomb of Lazarus had the Resurrection with them. They had the Alpha and Omega, the beginning and the end, right there, but what He saw was disbelief. So He wept.

Reviving the Dead

Without Jesus, we are dead and buried. We are dead in our finances, health, and relationships. We are buried in sorrow, grief, disappointment, heartbreak, and depression. The good news is that Jesus comes to the tomb.

Lazarus's tomb was a cave with a stone across the entrance. Not only are we dead and buried, but something heavy needs to be removed before we can be revived. There's a weight on our hearts and spirits that we can't remove. We can't be revived with it still weighing on us.

It may seem too difficult a task for us, but God can move that stone away.

> *"Take away the stone," he said.*
>
> *"But, Lord," said Martha, the sister of the dead man, "by this time there is a bad odor, for he has been there four days."*
> *—John 11:39*

The odor of the tomb would have knocked us back. The odor of a decaying man is unlike anything else—definitely far worse than your garbage can at the end of the week.

Jesus said, "Did I not tell you that if you believe, you will see the glory of God?" (John 11:40). The people were lamenting that the stone was too heavy and the odor was too bad. If they just believed, they would see the glory of God. We need to stop worrying about what we can't do ourselves and just believe. Then we will witness God roll away our stones and revive what is dead.

> *The dead man came out, his hands and feet wrapped with strips of linen, and a cloth around his face.*
>
> *Jesus said to them, "Take off the grave clothes and let him go."*
> *—John 11:44*

God wants you to remove that negative mindset. Remove the mindset that you'll never have another dime of this world's income. Remove the heartbreak that you can't seem to let go of. Take it off, lose it, and let it go.

Death has no authority when the King of kings is around. Dead things cannot survive when the living God says, "I am the resurrection."

> *"For I know the plans I have for you," declares the LORD, "plans to prosper you and not to harm you, plans to give you hope and a future."*
> —*Jeremiah 29:11*

This is the Lord saying, "I have a plan for you, and it's going to be a challenge beyond challenges." If you don't allow the resurrected Lord to resurrect the dead parts of your life, you'll never get to where He wants you to be. But if you believe in the Son of the living God, He will bring your heart and mind from death to life.

WORKBOOK

Chapter Nine Questions

Question: What is dead in your life right now that needs to be resurrected?

_____
_____
_____
_____
_____
_____
_____
_____
_____
_____

Question: What obstacles of unbelief are keeping you from having faith that God can revive the dead aspects of your life?

_____
_____
_____
_____
_____
_____
_____
_____
_____
_____

Action: Call upon the resurrected Lord. On a piece of paper, write a list of all the things you believe are too far gone for Christ to save. For each area of your life on that list, call upon Jesus. Ask Him to show up and bring what is dead to life.

Chapter Nine Notes

CHAPTER TEN

Sharing Jesus

Read Matthew 28:16–20.

Now, brothers and sisters, I want to remind you of the gospel I preached to you, which you received and on which you have taken your stand. By this gospel you are saved, if you hold firmly to the word I preached to you. Otherwise, you have believed in vain.

For what I received I passed on to you as of first importance: that Christ died for our sins according to the Scriptures, that he was buried, that he was raised on the third day according to the Scriptures, and that he appeared to Cephas, and then to the Twelve. After that, he appeared to more than five hundred of the brothers and sisters at the same time, most of whom are still living, though some have fallen asleep. Then he appeared to James, then to all the apostles, and last of all he appeared to me also, as to one abnormally born.

For I am the least of the apostles and do not even deserve to be called an apostle, because I persecuted the church of God.

—1 Corinthians 15:1–9

After Jesus rose, not only was He seen by the eleven (Judas had hanged himself at this point), but He was also seen by the five hundred. In Matthew 28, Jesus gave a commission to those who followed Him, and that's the same commission we have today.

Go and Share!

Jesus said to "go and make disciples of all nations" (Matthew 28:19). He gave us a command to go. Jesus wants us not only to receive the gospel message, enjoy God's blessings, and witness miracles in our lives, but also to share these things with "all nations"—men and women of all cultures, countries, and languages.

Taking Salvation for Granted

Some of us have gotten so comfortable in our Christian walk that we've stopped sharing. Not only have we stopped sharing by word, but we've stopped sharing by the way we live. We've developed a mistrust of God and His Word. If you don't love the Bible, you don't love God, because God is also His Word.

Are you still excited about your salvation? Are you still excited that Jesus is the one who woke you up this morning? Sometimes we take things for granted. We used to hear testimonies that spoke of how grateful people were that Jesus woke them up that morning. It seems as though those types of testimonies have gotten boring to us. When we wake up, we take it for granted.

In the book of Job, he prayed for his children. When

they began to party, he said, "Just in case they might have sinned against God, I'm going to pray for them" (Job 1:5, paraphrased). It didn't matter if they were fifteen or twenty-five. Job had a close connection with God, and he wanted God to watch over his children. Those types of prayers have gone by the wayside.

The Word of God has gotten boring to some believers. When we're not in the Word of God, asking Him for revelations, then we're not walking in the way God has asked us to walk.

The end times are coming, but Christians have shut their mouths. We'll speak up for a special occasion. We'll get political when something drastic happens. When a plane crashes, we'll come and pray. But when everyday life goes on as usual, we seem like we're waiting for a catastrophe to happen so we can spring into action.

We're waiting for something to happen, but the something we're waiting for has already happened. We turn our heads and try to ignore it. Believers need to know that God has everything under control and that every day is an opportunity to talk to someone, to bear witness to God's glory and love, and to show the world that God is still on the throne. Waking up in the morning and thanking God for that never gets old.

All Authority

> *Then Jesus came to them and said, "All authority in heaven and on earth has been given to me."*
> —*Matthew 28:18*

We're still in the process of discovery, but God has given us everything. Jesus has been given all authority, and He shares it with us. In light of His death and resurrection, we need to share what He has given us.

A Daily Walk

We've gotten so lazy in the United States that we've stopped going out as God told us to do. Instead, we expect the world to come to us.

Are you still going out and speaking the message, or are you waiting for catastrophe to strike before you move? Are you waiting for your neighbors to die before you do something? What were you doing before they lost their lives?

The Christian walk is a daily walk. It's a daily growing in the gospel message. If you stop sharing, you stop caring. If you stop caring, you have stopped reading the Word of God, because if you keep reading, it will tell you to keep witnessing. Our days are busy, but what's more important than saving people's lives and giving them hope in Jesus Christ? We need to get our priorities straight and stop making ourselves too busy to do the most important thing.

Baptizing in His Name

I was talking to a gentleman at the laundromat the other day. He looked at me and asked, "Are you a preacher?"

I said, "Yes, sir."

"Can I ask you a question? When you baptize, who do

you baptize in?"

I said, "The Father, the Son, and the Holy Ghost."

I believe that God was sending me a message. After I left the man's presence, I realized that more times than not, we make assumptions as believers that everybody knows what we're talking about. We don't explain it in a way other people understand. We get upset when people don't accept Christ, but what they're asking for is more information.

The man at the laundromat told me that the Bible says to baptize in the Holy Ghost. He got belligerent about it, and it seemed that I wasn't getting the point across to him or he wasn't listening to me. The truth was that I wasn't listening to God.

When folks tell you something and won't budge on it, don't get mad. Listen! Baptizing in the name of Jesus is essential for us to explain. We are saved by the name of Jesus. We confess in the name of Jesus. When we baptize in the name the Jesus, God agrees with His Word.

Jesus could have said to baptize people in the Father, the Son, and the Holy Ghost, but He didn't. He said, "Therefore go and make disciples of all nations, baptizing them *in the name of* the Father and of the Son and of the Holy Spirit, and teaching them to obey everything I have commanded you" (Matthew 28:19–20, emphasis added).

Start saying the name! God wouldn't have placed that detail there in the penmanship of Matthew if it weren't important. When we baptize people, sometimes we forget about Jesus. We just assume that people know what we mean. There are some people who haven't had the opportunity to see God's Word as we see it. Then we stop trying to go out and share, because we come up against this misunderstanding.

Are You Still Going?

How many people have you talked to about the Lord in the past week? How does your life display Jesus in the checkout line? How does your life display Jesus when you get a little upset? Can you still hold on to your Christian integrity when you're tired and stressed?

Jesus told His disciples, "Surely I am with you always, to the very end of the age" (Matthew 28:20). Everything we do in His name and according to His will has His stamp on it, and we need to be confident that He is right there with us always, even to the end of the world. His authority is with us. His love is with us. His kindness and compassion are with us. He gives us everything we need, and what He asks of us is to bear witness with our lives and share His gospel with the world.

Have you said to yourself, "I've reached my quota, so I'm stopping. I've done enough." There may be someone who wants a relationship with Jesus but doesn't know how to get there. I'm pretty sure that when you were saved, somebody told you about Jesus. You've experienced the Christ who saved you and transformed your life. Now go out and invite others to come home to Him.

WORKBOOK

Chapter Ten Questions

Question: Is sharing Christ with others a priority in your life and a natural overflow of your relationship with Him? Are you still excited about your salvation to the point of wanting others to experience life in Christ? How can you reinvigorate your passion for Christ?

_____

_____

_____

_____

_____

_____

_____

_____

_____

_____

Question: Is your relationship with Jesus a daily walk, or is it something you only think about on Sunday mornings at church? What steps can you take to make your relationship with Christ central to your daily reality?

_____

_____

_____

_____

_____

_____

_____

_____

_____

Action: Look for an opportunity to share the love of Jesus with someone. It may be someone who has already been on your heart and doesn't yet know Him, or maybe it's someone you'll meet while running errands or at work. Keep your heart and mind open to the Spirit's leading to share Jesus with those you encounter.

Chapter Ten Notes

CONCLUSION

On the Winning Side

I have a son named William. We used to watch sports together, and I would tell him to pick a winner before we even started. He would choose a side, but when his side seemed like it was going to lose, he'd switch.

When you recognize in your life that you're not on the winning side, will you decide to switch, or will you continue to lose? Will you continue to go your own way, take your own route, and choose your own direction, even when it's evident to you that something needs to change?

You've probably been in a situation a few times when you knew that it would be a good idea to do something different. But because of arrogance and stubbornness, you refused to change. We struggle with being on the winning side, and the Pharisees had this problem, too.

On the Losing Side

> *Meanwhile a large crowd of Jews found out that Jesus was there and came, not only because of him but also to see Lazarus, whom he had raised from the dead. So the chief priests made plans to kill Lazarus as well, for on account of him many of the Jews were going over to Jesus and believing in him.*
> —*John 12:9-11*

They were beginning to switch sides. They were beginning to see the writing on the wall. They were beginning to understand that there was a power greater than anything they had ever experienced before. They began to believe that Jesus was very powerful, and they wanted to be on His side.

The Pharisees, the court jesters, and the Sanhedrin knew that they had a problem. They didn't want to see Jesus as the Messiah, because He came from the virgin Mary. He didn't come from a palace. He was born in the red-light district. He was poor and didn't have an education. He didn't go to prestigious universities. He wasn't a great theologian or philosopher. He was Jesus! They knew His mother, brothers, and sisters. But they saw that these Jews were switching sides.

When you're part of a team or society and you begin to lose people, that makes you angry. When you lose folks, you lose support. When you lose support, you lose money. When someone puts out a product that's better than your product, you need to take that other product down so yours can go back into the limelight.

The Movement

> *The next day the great crowd that had come for the festival heard that Jesus was on his way to Jerusalem. They took palm branches and went out to meet him, shouting,*
>
> *"Hosanna!"*
>
> *"Blessed is he who comes in the name of the Lord!"*
>
> *"Blessed is the king of Israel!"*
>
> *Jesus found a young donkey and sat on it, as it is written:*
>
> *"Do not be afraid, Daughter Zion; see, your king is coming, seated on a donkey's colt."*
>
> —*John 12:12–15*

The Old Testament concealed, and the New Testament revealed. John 12:16 says, "At first his disciples did not understand all this. Only after Jesus was glorified did they realize that these things had been written about him and that these things had been done to him."

Sometimes when you're part of a movement, you don't realize how powerful it can be. We now understand how powerful the Civil Rights movement was, but not everyone knew at the time. We understand that things had to change and sides had to be taken, even to the point of death. It was a beneficial movement for the entire nation.

Jesus was making a movement. He was coming as promised in the Old Testament. He was going through the ridicule He needed to go through. He was proving Himself to be who He said He was.

The Pharisees and the Sanhedrin in that day didn't

want to believe Jesus. When your little mom and pop shop is going out of business and losing money to Walmart, you feel like you have to do something about it. So some of the religious leaders decided to kill Lazarus and Jesus. They figured that would cause the problem to go away.

Are You on the Winning Side?

> *Now the crowd that was with him when he called Lazarus from the tomb and raised him from the dead continued to spread the word. Many people, because they had heard that he had performed this sign, went out to meet him. So the Pharisees said to one another, "See, this is getting us nowhere. Look how the whole world has gone after him!"*
> —*John 12:17-19*

The Pharisees were on the losing side, and the signs were evident that the game was almost over. In fact, the game was already over, but they didn't have enough faith to switch sides. The question is: Are you on the winning side?

Jesus was paraded down that street. Palm leaves were on the ground. People shouted, "Hosanna!" and believed by faith that He was the side they needed to be on. What do you believe? You might have tried things other than Jesus. I know that I have.

Do you hold on to the ropes of a sinking ship, or do you go for the ship with working sails? Do you hold on to a life that you can see is dwindling and fading, or do you call upon the name of Jesus to rescue you and forgive you?

Open up your eyes and make sure that you're on the

winning side. Confess your thoughts to God and ask Him to forgive you of your sins. Romans 10:9 says, "If you declare with your mouth, 'Jesus is Lord,' and believe in your heart that God raised him from the dead, you will be saved."

Tell God that you're sorry. You've been trying to control your own life, and you see that you're not doing a very good job! If anybody tells you that when you come to Christ, all your problems will go away, that's not true. You'll still have challenges, but you'll have comfort through them. God will be there for you, and those challenges will help you to grow and trust in the Lord more. It's not too late to switch to the winning side!

REFERENCES

Notes

1. Brooks, Richard. "Colours and Their Meanings Around the World." K International. December 21, 2016. https://k-international.com/blog/color-meanings-around-the-world/.

2. Zodhiates, Spiros. *The Complete Word Study Dictionary New Testament*. AMG Publishers, 1998. Logos Bible Software.

3. Lee, Johnny. "Looking for Love." Track 9 on *Urban Cowboy*. Asylum Records, 1980, vinyl.

4. Hackford, Taylor, dir. *Ray*. Universal Pictures, 2004.

About the Author

Dr. Willie Bell Sublet Jr. attended Harry Stone Elementary in Dallas, Texas. After his parents separated, he moved with his father to Houston, Texas, and began attending Chatham Elementary. He attended Kashmere Senior High School until he moved back to Dallas in January 1975. In 1978, he graduated from Franklin D. Roosevelt High School.

Dr. Sublet spent the next four years at McMurry College, now McMurry University, in Abilene, Texas, where he played football. He graduated in 1982 with a General Business Degree.

Dr. Sublet accepted Christ in 1984. He received his call to preach in 1990 while at New El Bethel Baptist Church in Dallas, Texas, under the leadership of Pastor V. L. Warren. Dr. Sublet taught Sunday school for men, couples, and children, in addition to directing the male chorus, children's chorus, and senior chorus. He also attended the Southern Bible Institute during his time under Pastor Warren.

Dr. Sublet then served at Bible Way Bible Church in Dallas under the leadership of Dr. Eddie B. Lane, a professor at Dallas Theological Seminary. There Dr. Sublet taught the couples and men's ministries, and he sang with and directed the male chorus.

At Sure Foundation Bible Church in Dallas, under the leadership of Bishop Maurice Ricks, Dr. Sublet led and instructed teacher development while overseeing the Sunday school lessons for men, couples, and children. He also sang with and directed the male choir, directed the senior choir, and acted as director over the senior ministry.

From 2001 to 2008, Dr. Sublet pastored Miracle Temple Mission Church in Dallas. In 2008, he became the founding pastor of WE Community Fellowship, where he continues to serve.

Dr. Sublet has also worked with the police department in DeSoto, Texas, in a program called DPAC—DeSoto Police and Clergy. As part of the MOC, Ministers on Call, he assisted in domestic violence cases and homicides for ten years. He offered counseling and obtained any additional information that could help the police investigations.

Dr. Sublet is a grateful Paw Paw to his beautiful grandchildren. He thanks God every day for that blessing. He is also the caregiver for his 89-year-old mother, another blessing. Although he has not received all of his life experiences with open arms, he wouldn't change anything, because he knows that God has used everything that has happened to show him the man He wants him to be in this hour.

Made in the USA
Monee, IL
22 August 2021